MW01613683

EXPLORING NATURE AROUND THE YEAR
WINTER

EXPLORING NATURE AROUND THE YEAR

WINTER

BY DAVID WEBSTER
PICTURES BY BARBARA STEADMAN

JULIAN ⟨M⟩ MESSNER

Text copyright © 1989 by David Webster
Illustrations copyright © 1989 Barbara Steadman
All rights reserved including the right of reproduction
in whole or in part in any form.
Published by Julian
Messner, a division of Silver Burdett Press, Inc.,
Simon & Schuster, Inc., Prentice Hall Bldg.,
Englewood Cliffs, NJ 07632.

JULIAN MESSNER and colophon are trademarks of
Simon & Schuster, Inc.

Design by Malle N. Whitaker

Manufactured in the United States of America.

(Lib. ed.) 10 9 8 7 6 5 4 3 2
(Pbk. ed.) 10 9 8 7 6 5 4 3

Library of Congress Cataloging-in-Publication Data
Webster, David, 1930–
      Exploring nature around the year : winter / by
      David Webster; pictures by Barbara Steadman.
         p.   cm.
      Includes index.
      Summary: A collection of activities and projects
exploring nature in the winter.
      1. Nature study—Juvenile literature.   2. Winter—
Juvenile literature.   [1. Winter.   2. Nature
study.]   I. Steadman, Barbara, ill.   II. Title.
QH81.W4392   1989
ISBN 0-671-65861-1 (lib. bdg.)
ISBN 0-671-65986-3 (pbk.)
508—dc20   89-12318
                                                              CIP
                                                               AC

CONTENTS

What is your favorite season? Some people like spring best with warmer weather and the blooming of colorful flowers. Summer brings lots of playtime, bare feet, and swimming. Fall is a season of colorful leaves and cool, brisk weather. But some people think winter is the most interesting season of the year.

Have you ever wondered why winter is colder than summer? Many people think the earth is farther from the sun in winter. But the earth really is closer to the sun in winter. If so, why are winters colder?

7

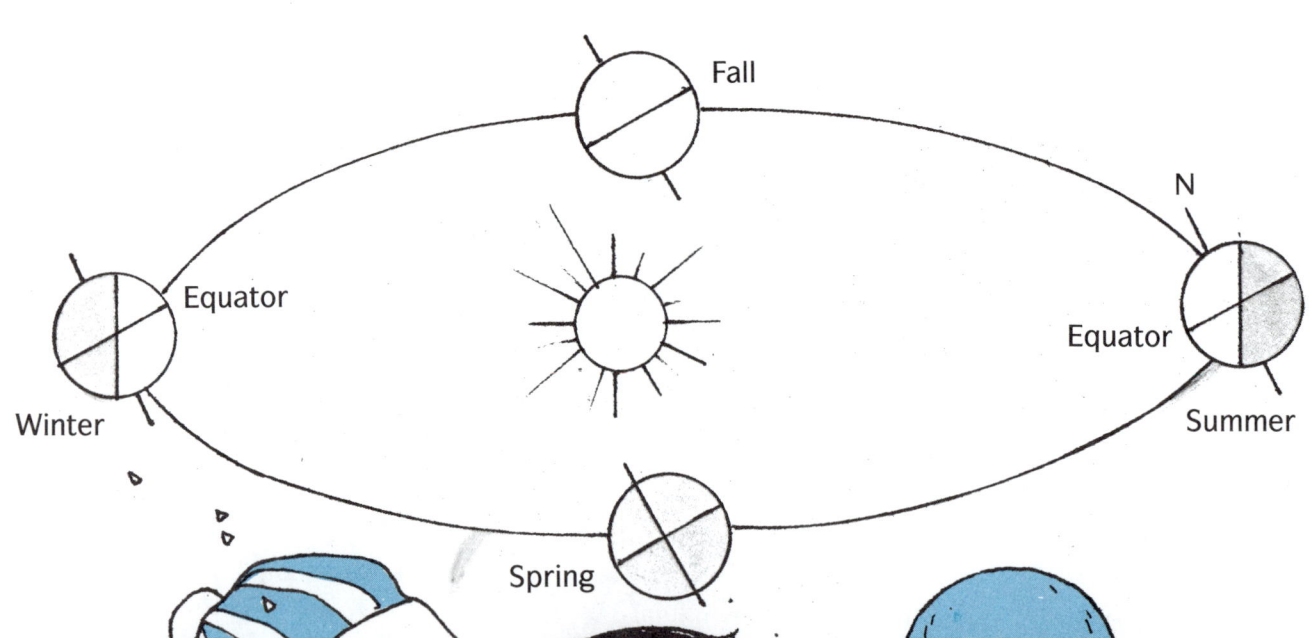

The seasons are caused by the way the earth moves around the sun. It takes a year for the earth to travel once around the sun. Because the earth is tilted, the Northern Hemisphere of the earth is tipped toward the sun in summer and away from the sun in winter.

In winter, when the Northern Hemisphere is tipped away from the sun, the days are shorter. Less sunlight means less heat. Also, the sun's rays are not as hot in the winter because they pass through more air before reaching the ground.

Now you can see why winter is colder and summer is warmer. If the earth were not tilted, there would not be different seasons.

Look at the drawing of the earth's orbit around the sun. Can you figure out why it is summer in South America at the same time it is winter in North America?

Winter's colder weather brings ice and snow in many places. Do you live where it snows every winter? If you live in parts of some states, such as Florida, Texas, and California, you may have never seen snow. In the north, snow may fall as early as October and it may not melt completely until May. Up there, a December snowman might last until spring!

Winter is a hard time for animals that live outside. Unlike you, animals cannot wear mittens and boots or sleep in a warm house. Food is much harder to find, too.

Most plants lose their leaves and stop growing during the winter months.

Winter is a great time of year to explore nature. There are many unusual things to see and do. This book will help you find out about things like the sun, snow and ice, and birds and trees in the winter.

THE HOT SUN

The sun is a gigantic ball of burning gases. Its fire is so hot that some of the heat travels all the way to earth, a distance of 93,000,000 miles.

The sun in the winter never feels as hot as it does in the summer. But you can use a magnifying glass to feel the heat of the winter sun. Perhaps your father or mother has a glass magnifier you can borrow. Small plastic magnifiers are not too expensive to buy.

Take a magnifying glass outside on a sunny day. Keep one hand facing the sun while you hold the magnifier about three inches in front of it. Slowly move the magnifier back and forth until the sun spot on your hand is as small as possible. Do you feel a little heat? *Never do this in the summer because you would burn your hand*.

Now tip your hand slowly to make the sunlight strike it at an angle. You should notice the spot on your hand becoming larger and not as hot. This is what happens during the winter: The sunlight strikes the earth at an angle. In the summer, the sunlight travels a straighter path to the earth.

THE BRIGHT SUN

The sun's fire is so bright that it lights up the whole world. When sunlight hits something shiny, the light is reflected. You can reflect the sun in many directions with a small mirror.

Go outside, face the sun, and slowly move the mirror until you see a bright spot of reflected light. Practice aiming the spot of light at different things. Can you shine light into a house window and see it on a wall inside? In what direction are you unable to reflect the sun? *Be careful not to reflect the sun into someone's eyes.*

Sunlight can be changed into electricity with solar cells. Space satellites use solar energy to run their computers and cameras. Maybe someday you will drive a car powered by the sun!

THE SUN IS A CLOCK

Before clocks were invented, some people used the sun to tell time. A sun clock is called a sundial. Here is how you can make a simple sundial:

1. Get a large piece of cardboard; place it on the ground in a spot that is in the sun all day.

2. Weight the corners of the cardboard with small rocks so the wind does not move it.

3. Push a pencil through the middle of the cardboard so it sticks up straight.

4. At nine o'clock in the morning, trace over the pencil's shadow with another pencil.

5. Mark the line with the hour.

6. Try to draw the shadow every hour until three or four o'clock in the afternoon.

7. Do not move the cardboard when you are done.

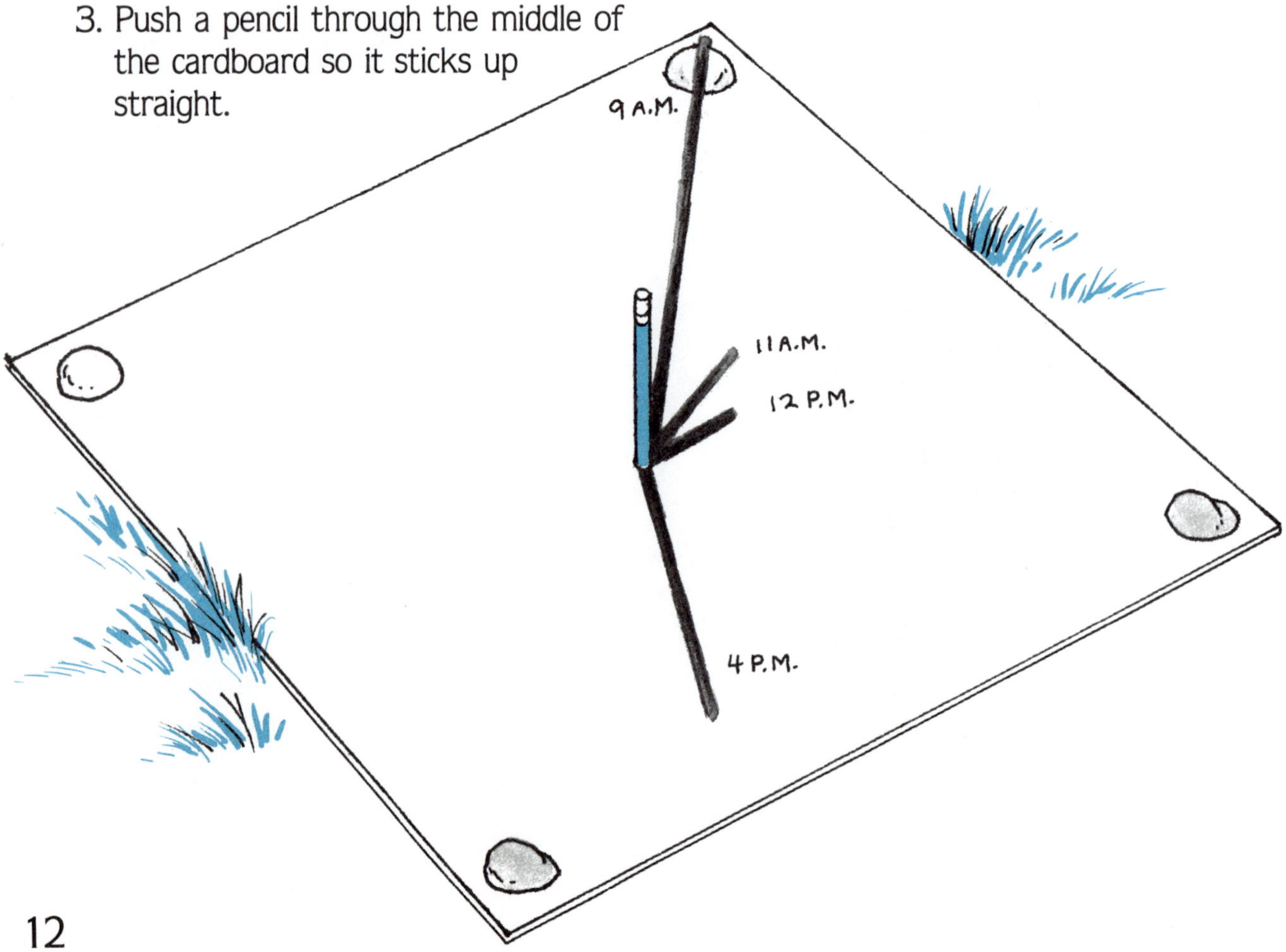

9 A.M.

11 A.M.

12 P.M.

4 P.M.

If the next day is sunny, you should be able to tell the time with your sundial. Is it noon when the pencil's shadow again falls on the twelve o'clock line? What is the time if the pencil's shadow is halfway between the marks for two o'clock and three o'clock? When is the shadow the longest?

After a few days, your pencil sundial will no longer tell the right time. This is because the height of the sun changes a little every day. The stick on a real sundial must be set at a certain angle. The drawing shows what one looks like. In what ways is a watch better than a sundial?

A long time ago, people thought the sun moved across the sky every day. Now we know that the sun does not move around the earth. It is the turning earth that makes it look as if the sun is moving.

THE SUN IS A COMPASS

The sun can be used as a compass. The sun rises from the east, is high toward the south at noon, and then sets in the west. This means you can use the sun to find directions.

Draw a compass face on a piece of cardboard. Take the cardboard outside on a sunny day at noon. Stick a pencil into the ground; then turn your compass face until the shadow of the pencil covers the south line. Now all the compass points are aiming in the right direction. Hold the compass face in place with a few small rocks.

Check your sun compass later in the afternoon. Has the sun moved toward the west? Look again in the morning. Does the sun rise exactly in the east, or somewhere between east and south?

The winter sun does not get as high in the sky as the summer sun. In winter there are only about ten to eleven hours of daylight; in the early summer it is light for more than fifteen hours.

14

SHADOWS

On a sunny winter day, go for a Shadow Walk. All kinds of shadows are easy to find. The leaves on bushes and trees often make shadows with holes. Look for moving shadows. Does air make any shadow?

Watch your own shadow as you walk in the sun. The only way to get away from your shadow is to jump off the ground. Where can you stand so that you have no shadow?

Try to make your shadow look like a monster. Can you make a shadow that has no head or a shadow with very short arms?

What is the largest shadow you have seen? Maybe you think of tree shadows or house shadows. But the biggest shadow is the earth's shadow at night.

The earth slowly spins around and around like a giant top. When you are on the side of the earth facing the sun, it is daytime. At night, your side of the earth is facing away from the sun. Can you figure out how long it takes for the earth to turn around once?

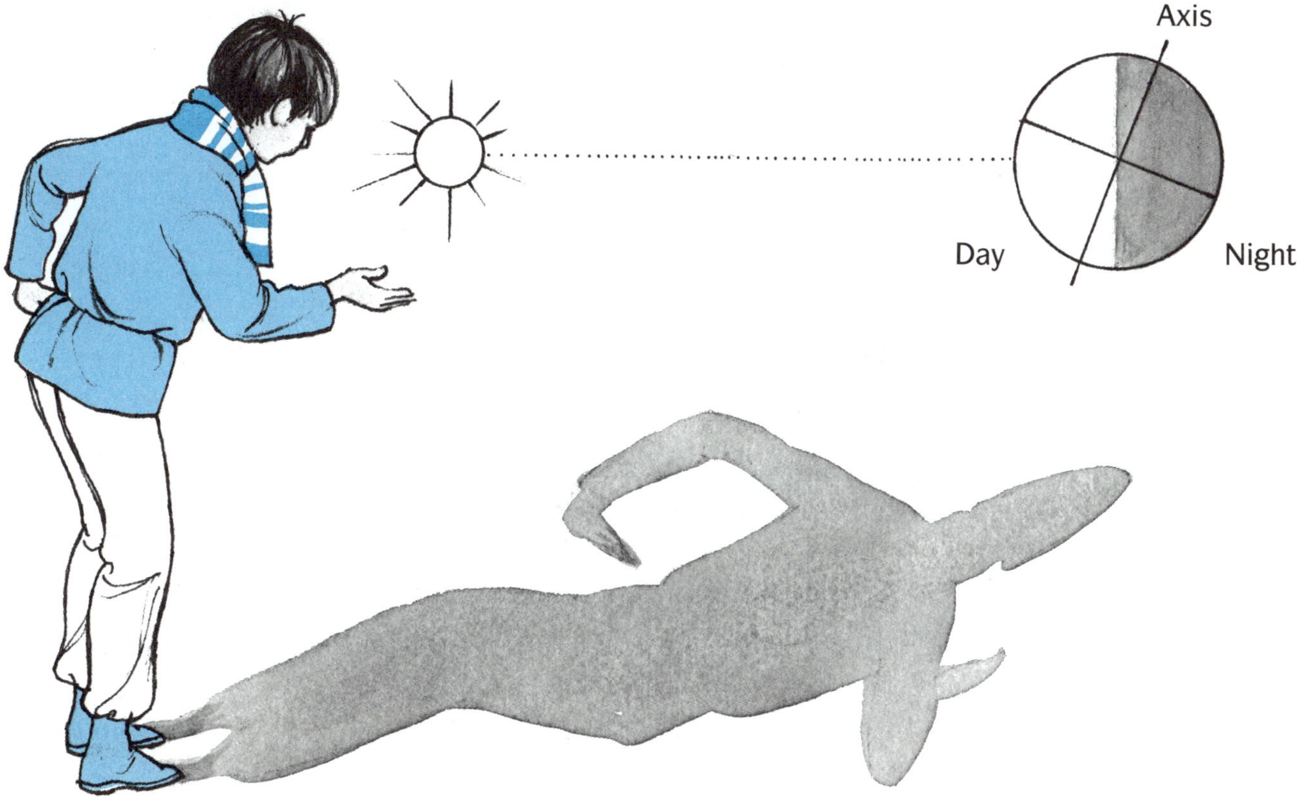

Axis

Day

Night

THE GREAT SNOWBALL MYSTERY

Here is a trick you can do with a melting snowball.

Make a firm snowball and push it on the end of a two-foot stick. Indoors, rest the snowball over a table edge and hold down the end of the stick with a heavy book. Put a pan on the floor under the snowball.

Now ask people to guess how long it will take for the first drop of water to fall into the pan as the snowball melts. Most people will guess a short time, maybe one or two minutes. What is your guess? Then ask them to guess how long it will take for the whole snowball to melt.

Keep watching the snowball until a drop of water falls. You will be surprised at how long it takes.

The snowball does begin to melt almost as soon as you bring it inside. Instead of dripping off, though, the water sticks to the unmelted snow. Snow is somewhat like a sponge; it can hold a lot of water.

Note: If it does not snow where you live, you can make "snow" from ice cubes. Ask an adult to help you crush ice cubes in a food processor. Or you can crush ice in a metal bucket by pounding it with the end of a hammer handle.

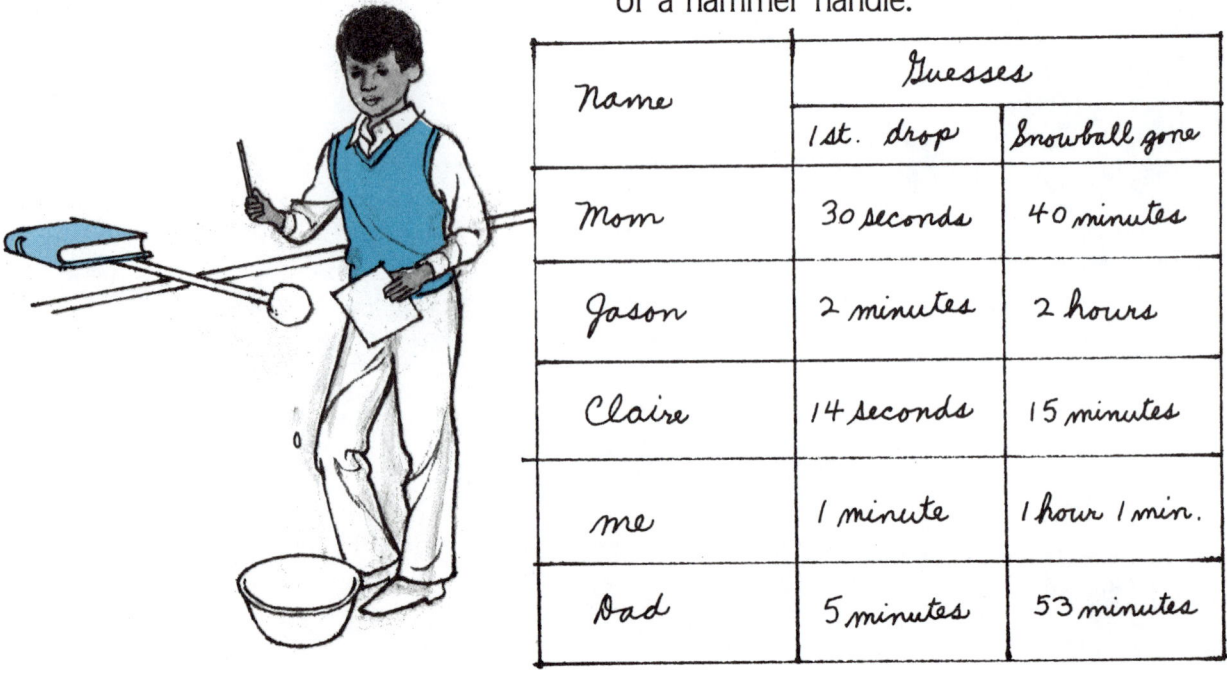

Name	Guesses	
	1st. drop	Snowball gone
Mom	30 seconds	40 minutes
Jason	2 minutes	2 hours
Claire	14 seconds	15 minutes
me	1 minute	1 hour 1 min.
Dad	5 minutes	53 minutes

HOW TO KEEP SNOW FROM MELTING

Think about places you could put a cup of snow to keep it from melting. Of course snow melts slower in cold places, such as a refrigerator. But can you make snow melt slower in warm places?

Fill five or six paper cups with snow and put them in different places. If you have no snow, use ice cubes instead. You could put one cup of snow in the refrigerator and another cup in the freezer. Wrap the third cup of snow in a large towel. Try some ideas of your own for the other cups.

Look at the snow cups every hour and write down the results of your melting experiment. Remember to note the time you started.

The snow inside the towel melted more slowly because it was insulated. The warm air took longer to pass through the towel and melt the snow. Your house has insulation in the walls and roof to help hold the heat inside.

Time started _____	
Location of snow cups	Time to melt completely
Outside house	
In refrigerator	
In freezer	
Wrapped in towel	
Window sill - no sun	
In dark closet	

MELTING SNOW FASTER

You probably know that rock salt is used to melt snow on highways and sidewalks. Table salt does the same thing. Get two cups of snow (or ice cubes), and dump a lot of salt on the snow in one cup. Does the salted snow melt faster?

Snow melts outside even on cold days. Put a small rock on top of some snow outside, and leave it for a few days. You will notice that it melts down into the snow. The rock absorbs heat from the sun and air.

Dark colors absorb more heat than light colors. You can show this with colored paper. Cut out one square of white paper and another from dark paper. Place the squares on top of some snow in the sun.

Look at the squares after a few hours. Why has more snow melted under the dark square? Why do people who live in hot desert countries wear white clothing?

If there is no snow, put a penny on an ice cube and place it in the sun. Does the coin melt into the ice?

SNOW WATER

Here is another science puzzle: How much water comes from melted snow?

Get a tall glass and fill it to the top with loose snow. If there is no snow, you can use crushed ice. Attach a ruler to the side of the glass with a rubber band.

Have everyone, including yourself, guess how much water will be in the glass after all the snow melts. Write the guesses on a piece of paper so you can check them later.

How much water came from the snow?

If you melted fluffy, new snow, there may be only one or two inches of water. Older snow becomes heavier and might make four or five inches of water. Do the experiment another day with a different kind of snow.

Much of the water that fills lakes and reservoirs comes from melting snow. Sometimes, when snow melts too quickly, there are spring floods. Weather scientists need to know how much water is in the snow.

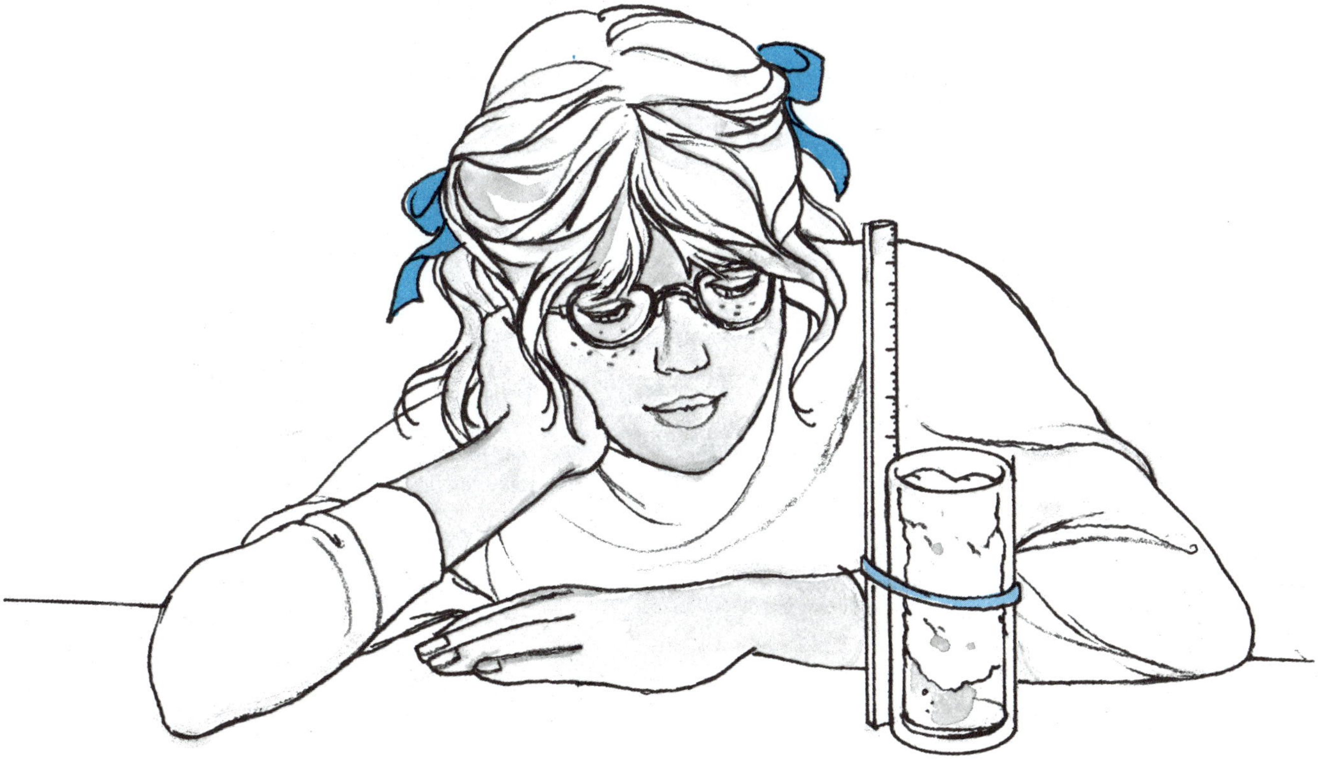

DIRTY SNOW

Usually snow looks white and clean. But even fresh snow has some dirt in it that you cannot see.

To see snow dirt, first melt a pan of snow inside your house. The snow will melt much faster if you set the pan on a radiator or heat vent.

Cover the top of a large glass or jar with a white paper towel. Hold the towel in place with a rubber band. Slowly pour the snow water from the pan through the towel. Some of the dirt from the snow will be caught in the paper towel. Can you see any dirt?

Dust in the air gets stuck to snowflakes before they hit the ground. More dust and dirt collects on snow after it has fallen. Old snow often looks dirtier as it melts. It is not a good idea to eat snow, since you can never be sure how much dirt is in it.

SNOW GOGGLES

Bright sunlight reflecting from snow can hurt your eyes. Eskimos invented slitted snow goggles to wear in the sun.

You can make a pair of Eskimo goggles to use on a bright winter day. You will need:

a piece of heavy cardboard about six inches long

pencil, ruler, and scissors

thin rubber bands

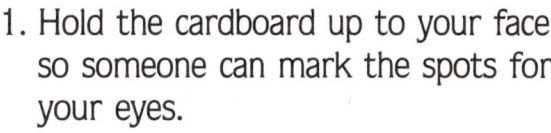

1. Hold the cardboard up to your face so someone can mark the spots for your eyes.

2. Use the pencil and ruler to draw two narrow slits.

3. Cut out the slits and make a notch for your nose.

4. Poke a hole on each side.

5. Tie rubber bands together to make a head band.

Put on your snow goggles and look in a mirror. Then try them outside. Take off the goggles and see if the bright sun makes you squint.

THE POWER OF ICE

What is the temperature of snow? It is 32°F. This is also the temperature at which water freezes and changes into ice. A strange thing happens to water when it freezes: it gets larger. This increase in size is called expansion.

You can see how much ice expands with a plastic container, such as a milk jug or a plastic soda bottle. The container must have a screw cap. Fill it to the top with water and tighten the cap. You can freeze the water outside if the temperature at night gets below 32°F. If not, leave the water container in your freezer overnight.

Look at the frozen container the next day. Has the expanded ice pushed out the sides? Perhaps the freezing force will have split open the plastic.

Anti-freeze is used to stop water from freezing. If the water in a car radiator is not mixed with anti-freeze during the cold winter, the water will freeze and break the radiator.

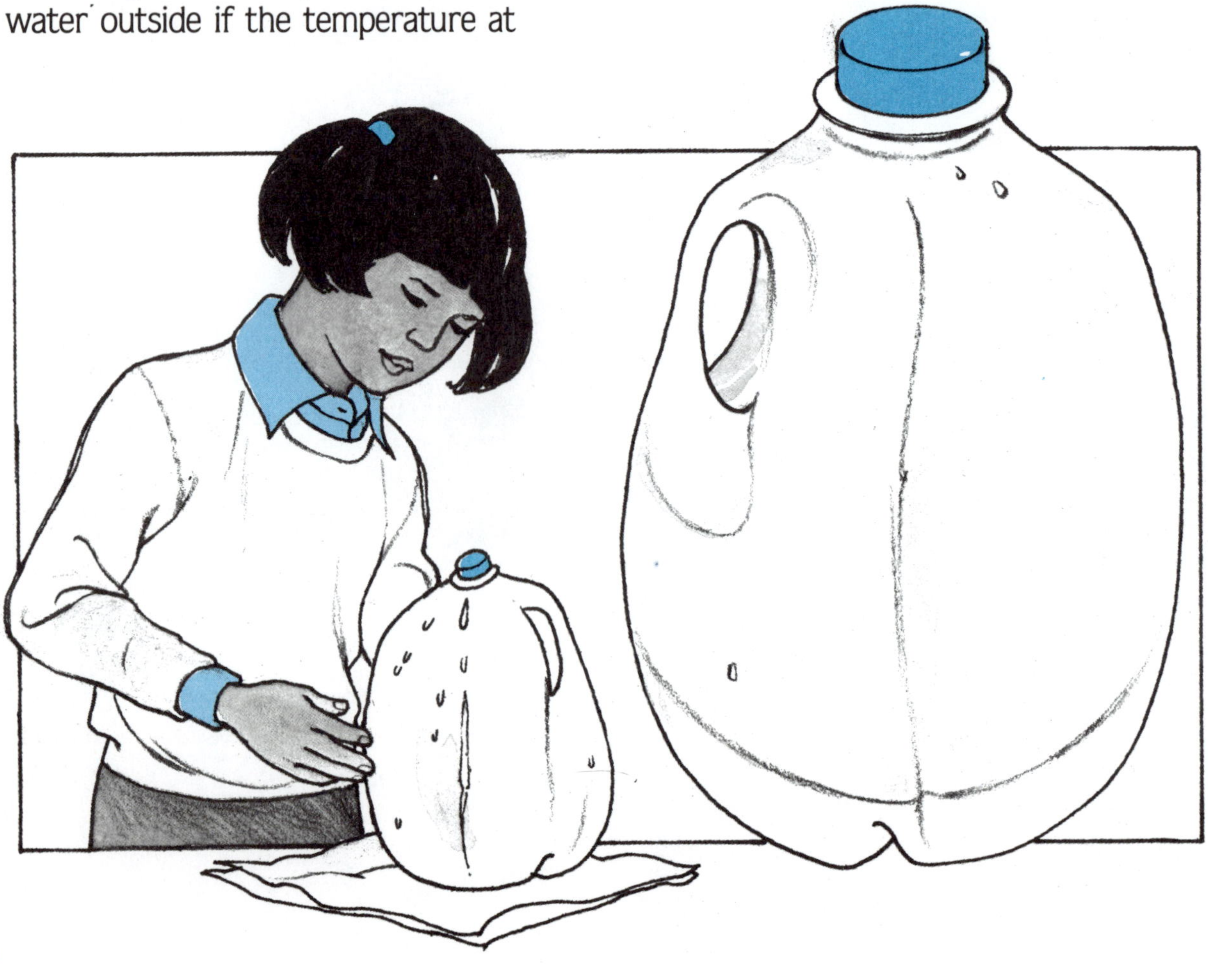

SNOW LIGHTS

In Germany, children make pretty "snow lights" that glow with color. You can make snow lights outdoors.

To make a snow light, you will need colored water. Put two cups of water in a pan and add enough red food coloring to turn the water dark red. Make blue and green water the same way in other pans.

Now make about twenty-five snowballs. Color the snowballs by dipping them into the pails of colored water. Make eight or nine snowballs of each color. Pile the snowballs up so there is an opening to a space inside. Your pile should look like a little colored igloo.

In Germany, a candle is used for light. The flame is not hot enough to melt the snow too quickly. You should not use a candle unless an adult helps. A flashlight or a light bulb on an extension cord is safer than a candle. You must wait until dark to see how your snow light shines.

ICE CASTLES

Have you ever made sand castles at the beach? In most places it is too cold in the winter for sand castles. Instead, you can create an ice castle.

For building blocks you will need to freeze water into different icy shapes. Find some plastic or metal molds, such as a baking tray, a cupcake tin, and food containers. Since water expands as it freezes, you cannot use any glass molds, which might break. Ask an adult which containers you may use.

1. Fill the molds with water. Add food coloring if you want colored blocks.

2. Leave the molds outside or in the freezer overnight. Of course, the temperature must go below 32°F. for ice to be formed.

3. The next morning, remove the ice shapes by dipping the molds into a bucket of water.

4. Scrape away the snow where the ground is flat and build your castle. The blocks can be stuck together with slush: a thick mixture of snow or crushed ice and water. Try to find some icicles to use for spires.

Remember to look at your castle every day as it begins to melt. How long will it last?

BE A TRACK DETECTIVE

Detectives solve crimes by studying clues. You can be a track detective and solve animal mysteries.

You can almost always find animal tracks in the snow, but the best time to look is after a light snowfall. Most of the tracks around your house probably are made by cats and dogs. Other tracks might be left by squirrels, pigeons, or other birds.

It is not hard to tell the difference between dog tracks and cat tracks. Most dog tracks are larger than cat tracks. Dog tracks have toenail marks, but cat tracks do not. This is because a cat's claws are pulled up so they do not touch the ground and get dull. Also, a walking dog leaves tracks in pairs.

Another thing tracks can tell you is whether an animal was walking, running, or hopping. The tracks of a walking dog are close together. But when a dog runs, it leaves sets of four tracks with long spaces in between.

Look at the track drawings. Which tracks were made by a walking dog? Which were made by a running dog? Which animal was hopping?

When you see tracks in the snow, try to figure out how the animal was moving.

Dog

Cat

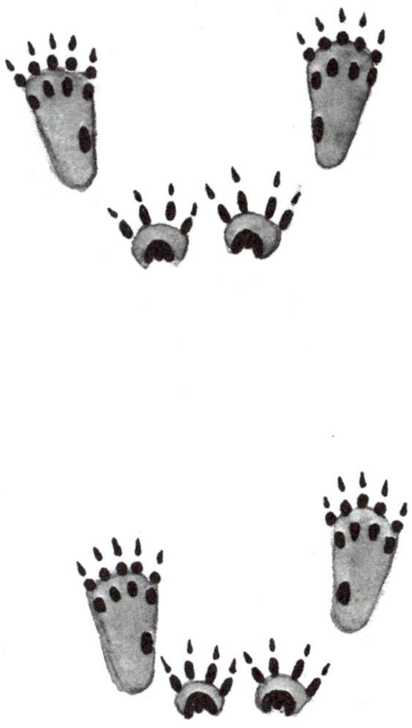

Squirrel

Dog

27

People tracks are even easier to find than animal tracks. The size of the footprint is a clue to the person's size. If snow conditions are right, the tread patterns on shoe soles show in the footprints.

You can play a track game with a friend. Ask your friend not to watch while you make some mystery tracks in the snow. You could hop on one foot, walk backwards, or step in the tracks of someone else. Then see if your friend can figure out what you did by looking at your tracks. Next time you can close your eyes while your friend makes tracks.

The American Indians were expert trackers. They knew how to follow the tracks of warriors from unfriendly tribes. When hunting game, Indians could follow the tracks of deer and other animals they needed for food.

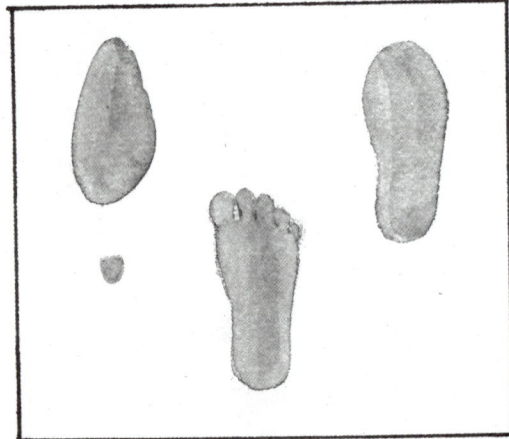

SNOW DEPTH

Weather stations use a depth gauge to measure how much snow falls. All you need to measure snow is a yardstick.

When it stops snowing, use the yardstick to measure how much snow has fallen. Go to an open area that is not near a building or trees. Push the yardstick straight down until it hits the ground. After reading the inches, shovel away the snow until you have a bare spot so you can measure the next snowfall.

Make a chart and write down the date and depth of every snowstorm during the winter. Listen to weather reports and compare their snow depths with your own measurements.

Date	Snow Depth	Kind of Snow
Nov. 15	2 inches	Wet
Dec. 7	6 inches	Fluffy
Dec. 25	2 inches	Slush
Jan. 11	4 inches	Heavy
Jan. 26 - 27	$13\frac{1}{2}$ inches	Fluffy

PLEASE FEED THE BIRDS

Sparrow

Chickadee

Woodpecker

Seed-eating Beak

Cardinal

Think how hard it would be if you were a bird and had to live in a tree all winter. Your down feathers would insulate your tiny body from the cold, but food would be very scarce. Most seeds would have dropped from the plants and now would be covered with snow.

You can help the winter birds by supplying them with food. Juncos, sparrows, cardinals, and chickadees eat seeds and raisins. Chickadees, woodpeckers, and nuthatches like fat and cheese. On the next pages are some ideas for making bird feeders.

It would be impossible for robins to dig worms from the hard, frozen ground. Swallows eat only flying insects, but these disappear during the winter. Birds such as robins and swallows migrate for the winter to warmer places where they can find food.

30

BIRD FEEDERS YOU CAN MAKE

The simplest feeder is just a metal or wooden tray for seed. The tray keeps the seed from getting damp or lost in the snow. You can make a wooden tray by nailing low sides around the edge of a short piece of wood.

Some birds like to feed in a tree rather than on the ground. For them, you will need a hanging feeder. The drawings show how to make hanging feeders from a jar cap or a milk carton.

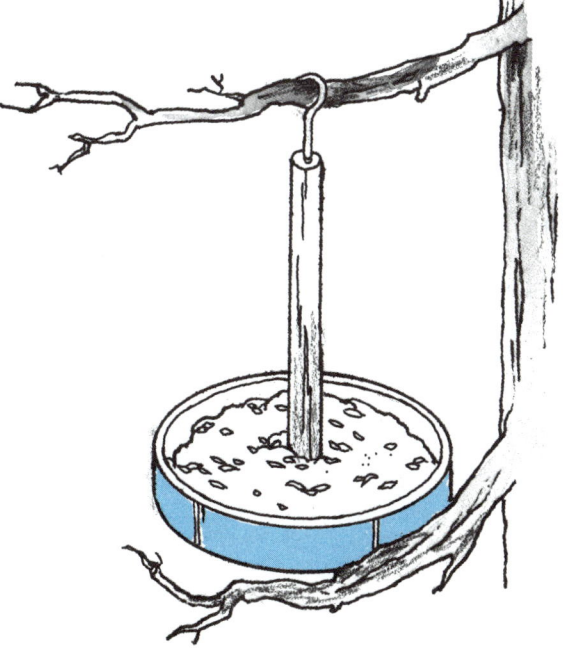

Many birds like suet, a hard fat you can buy at the meat department in a supermarket. Cheese or peanut butter can be used instead of suet. The drawings show two kinds of suet feeders.

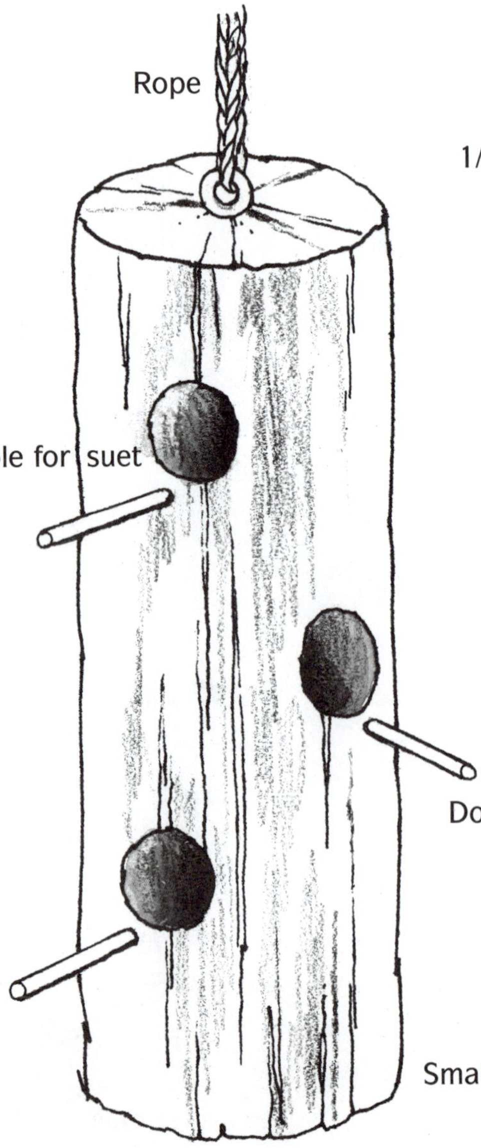

Rope

Nail

1/4" hardware cloth

Hole for suet

Wood

Dowel for perch

Small log

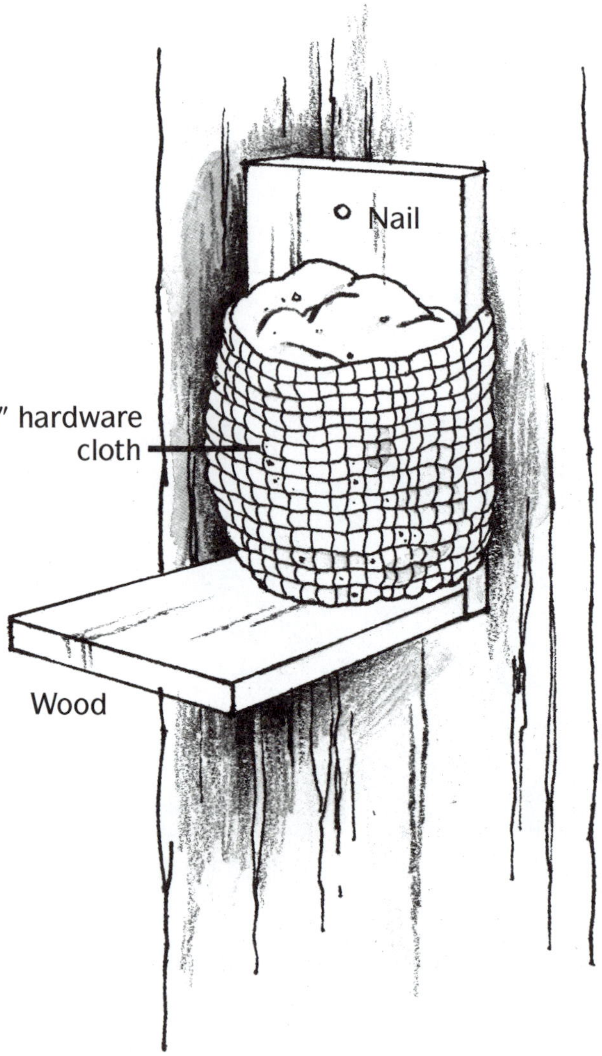

The best place to hang your feeder is in a bush or small tree. Birds feel safer eating close to shelter where they can hide from enemies. The feeder should be low enough for you to put in more food. However, be sure the feeder is high enough to keep cats from catching the birds. Try to put the feeder in a spot where you can see it from inside your house. It is fun to watch the birds eat.

Do not be upset if birds do not come to your feeder right away. It may take them a few days to find it. If no birds come in a week, hang it in a different place.

Once you begin feeding birds, you should continue for the rest of the winter until early spring. Birds learn to depend on your food and might starve if the feeder is empty.

Maybe squirrels will eat all the seed in your feeder before the birds get any. It is hard to keep squirrels away. But squirrels need winter food, too.

A CHRISTMAS TREE FEEDER

Usually old Christmas trees end up in the trash. Instead, you can redecorate your tree with holiday goodies for the birds.

Take the tree outside and tie it up against the trunk of a tree in your yard. If you don't tie up the tree, it will be blown over by the wind.

There are many foods you can hang on the birds' Christmas tree. Make chains of popcorn and cranberries threaded on strings. Stuff dried pine cones with peanut butter. Use colored ribbon to tie on donuts, knotted pretzels, and cookies.

Colorful seed baskets can be made from oranges. Cut off the top third of an orange. Scoop out the bottom part to leave the skin as a little cup. Poke holes around the edge. Then tie the orange skin cup to a branch and fill it with bird seed from the supermarket.

As soon as the birds find your tree, they will enjoy their holiday treats.

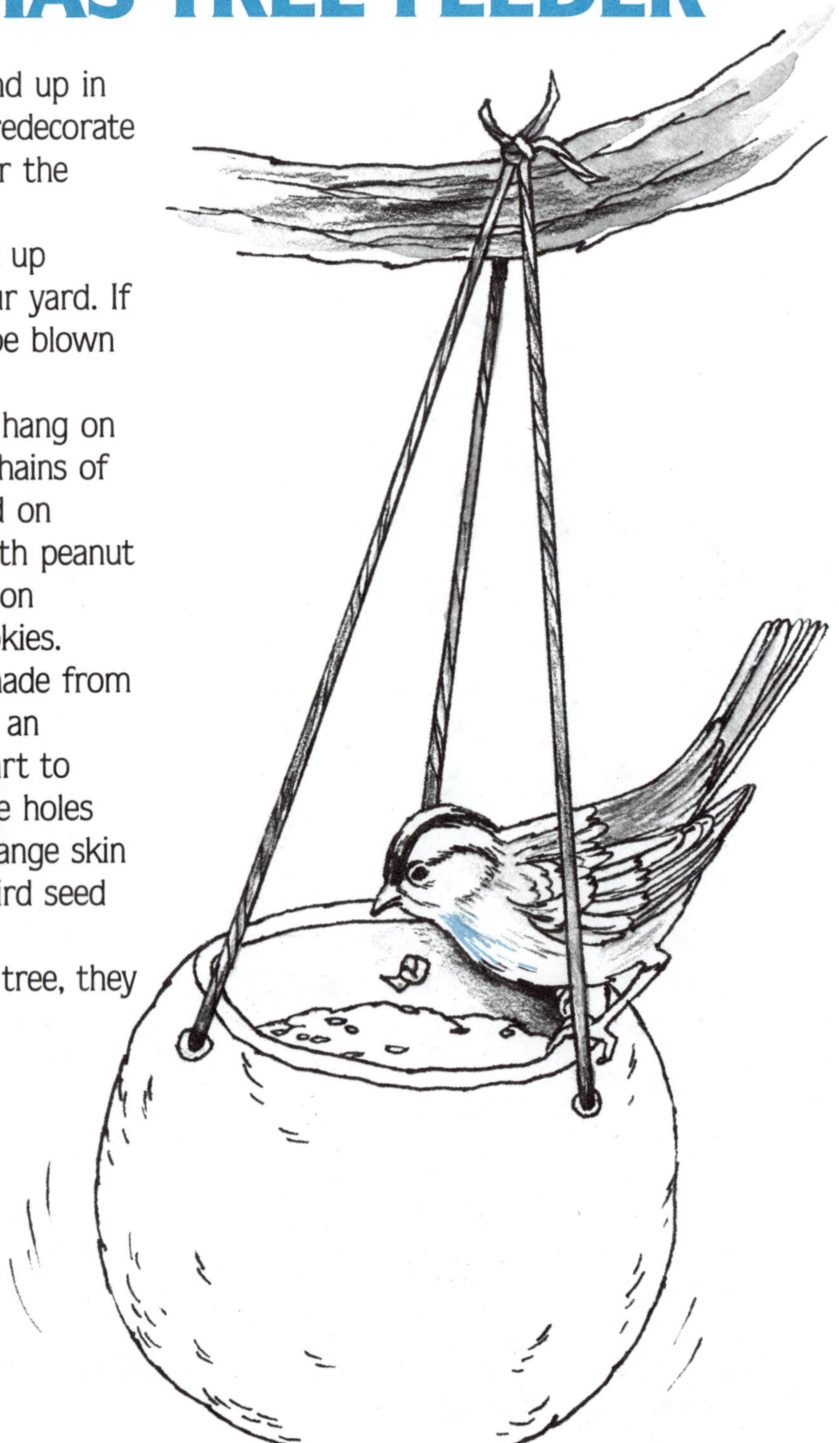

BIRDS NEED WATER

Just like you, birds need water to drink. Water is hard to find in the winter if the temperature is below freezing; the water freezes into ice.

Birds also need water for taking a bath. Dirty feathers stick together and leave patches of bare skin with no protection from the cold. Birds bathe even when the temperature is close to freezing.

For a bird bath you could use a large pan from the kitchen or a plastic trash can lid. Check the bird bath every day to see if the water has frozen. If this happens, break out the ice and add fresh water. The ice might thaw out during the day if the bath is placed in a sunny spot.

BIRD TRACKS

When birds visit your ground feeder, they may leave their footprints in the snow. If the ground is bare, you can still get bird tracks by spreading some flour. Put the seed tray in the middle of a larger board or piece of cardboard. Then sprinkle a thin layer of flour or baking soda on the board. Flour spread on the ground will become damp and not make good tracks.

Most birds have four toes on each foot. Birds that spend most of the time walking or hopping in the ground have three long toes in front and a shorter toe in back. Birds that scratch the ground in search of food have large toenails.

Woodpeckers and nuthatches have a different type of toe arrangement: two toes in front and two toes in back. Toes like this help the bird grip tree trunks as it searches for insects under the bark.

What kind of bird tracks would you expect to find around your seed tray?

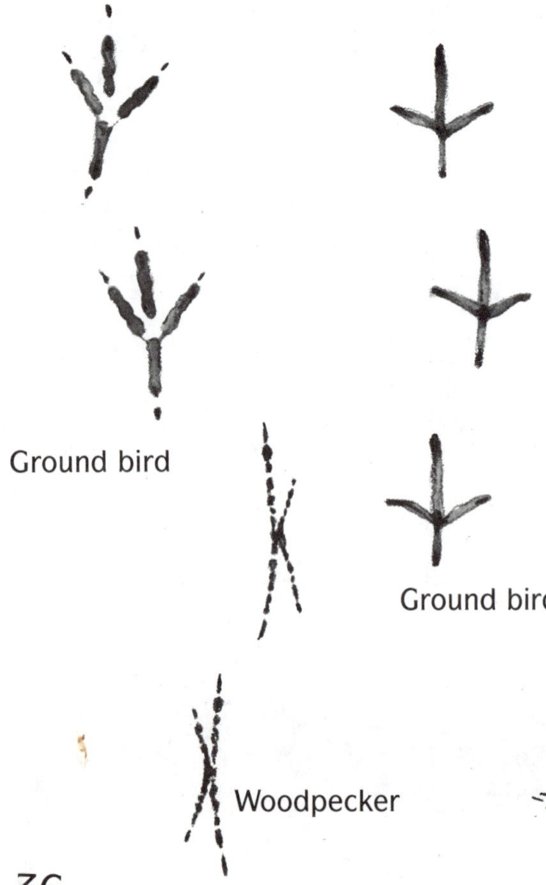

Ground bird

Ground bird

Woodpecker

36

FEATHERS

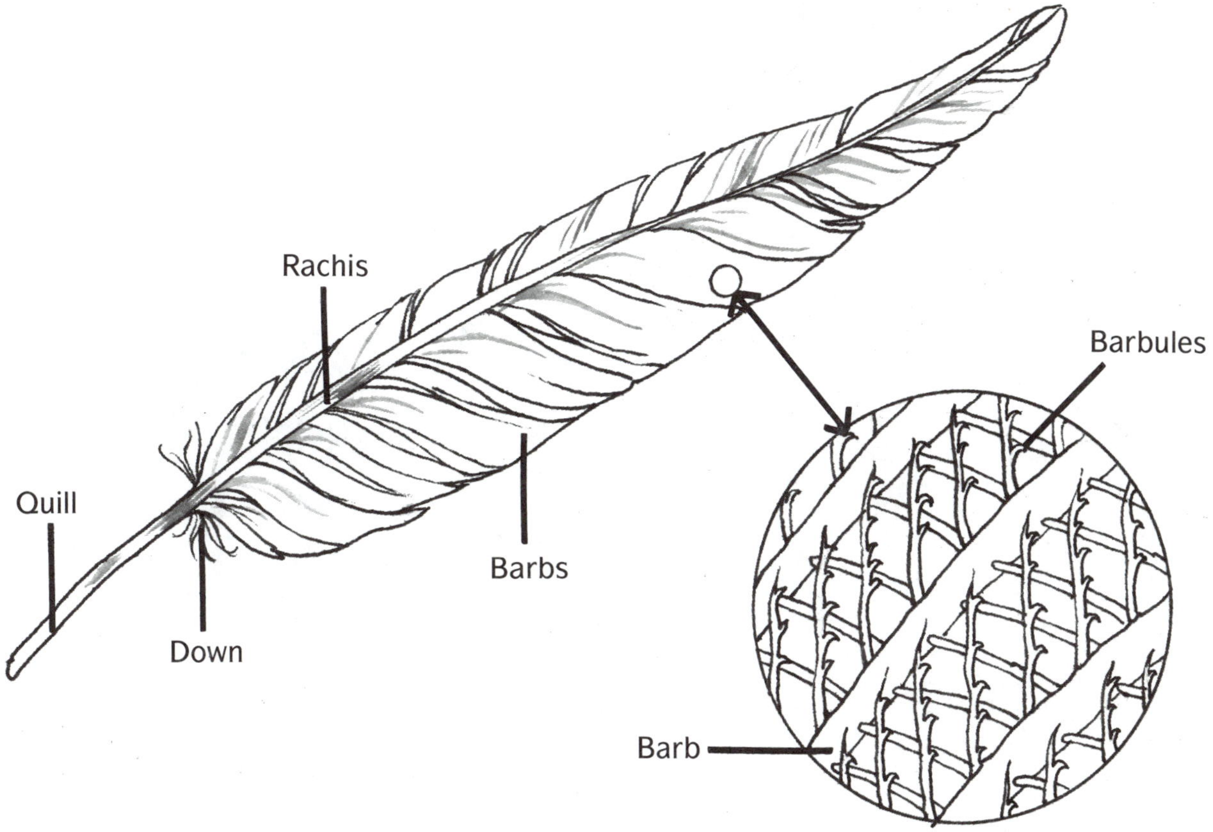

Rachis

Barbules

Quill

Barbs

Down

Barb

Birds occasionally lose a feather, especially when landing and taking off. If you are lucky, you will find a feather near your feeder. Or you might find a feather on the ground when you are out walking.

A feather has three main parts. The feather shaft is the hollow rachis. Attached to the rachis are barbs that form the flat surfaces used for flying. The fuzzy part near the bottom of the feather is down, which helps to keep the bird warm.

Look at the barbs with a magnifying glass. You should see thousands of tiny spikes along the barbs. These are called barbules and they make the barbs stick together.

Do you have any clothes with Velcro fasteners? The inventors of Velcro got their idea from barbules on bird feathers!

37

TREE BUDS

You may think that trees do not have leaves during the winter. The old leaves did fall off in the fall, and new leaves will not appear until spring. But trees have leaves in the winter even though you do not see them. The leaves are tiny and are hidden inside buds.

Go outside and gather small twigs from several different kinds of trees. Ask permission before you start, and get an adult to help you if you need to use a knife. Try to find some trees or bushes that have large buds.

Take the twigs inside and pick off a nice bud. A magnifying glass will help you study it. At first you will not see any leaves, because they are covered with brown scales. The scales protect the bud from cold temperatures, injury, and insects.

Pick off the scales with your fingernails or a pin. Underneath you should find very tiny leaves waiting to bloom. About how many baby leaves are in the bud?

Open buds from other twigs in the same way. How do buds differ?

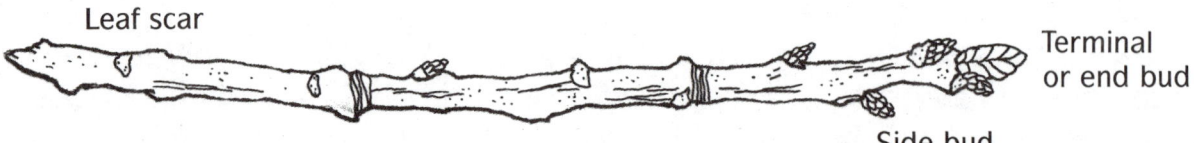

Leaf scar

Terminal or end bud

Side bud

FUNNY FACES

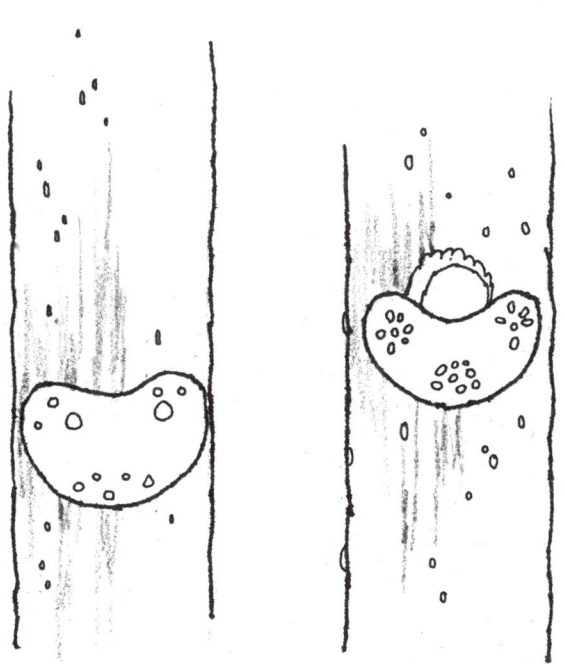

Do you notice any little faces on the twigs? With a magnifying glass, look at the lower part of a twig for small, circular marks. These are leaf scars which are left when old leaves drop off in the fall. The dots on the scar are the remains of pipelines that carried food and water between the twig and the leaf. Often these dots form the eyes, nose, and mouth for a leaf scar "face."

Look for leaf scar faces on the twigs you gathered. Do some scars remind you of grinning elves or mean monkeys? Maybe you can find a laughing gremlin or a spooky ghost.

See if you can make a drawing of an interesting leaf scar face. Color in the eyes and mouth with crayons. Add hair and ears to make the leaf scar look more like a real face.

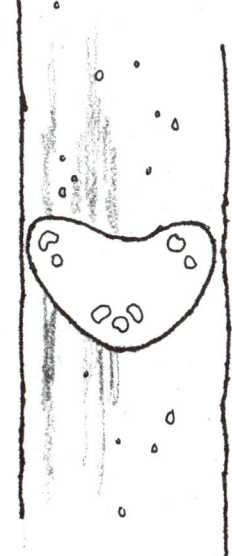

COLLECTING TWIGS

Willow

Maple

Elm

Spruce

Do you have any science collections? Some young scientists collect rocks or shells or butterflies. You can make a twig collection.

A garden pruner is the best tool for snipping off small twigs; a pair of kitchen scissors can also be used. Both of these are safer than a pocket knife.

You should try to collect a nice twig from five to ten different trees. Begin with trees near your house and then look for others around your school or in a park. Be sure to ask permission before you cut a twig from any tree.

It is nice to know the names of the trees from which you gather twigs. Ask an

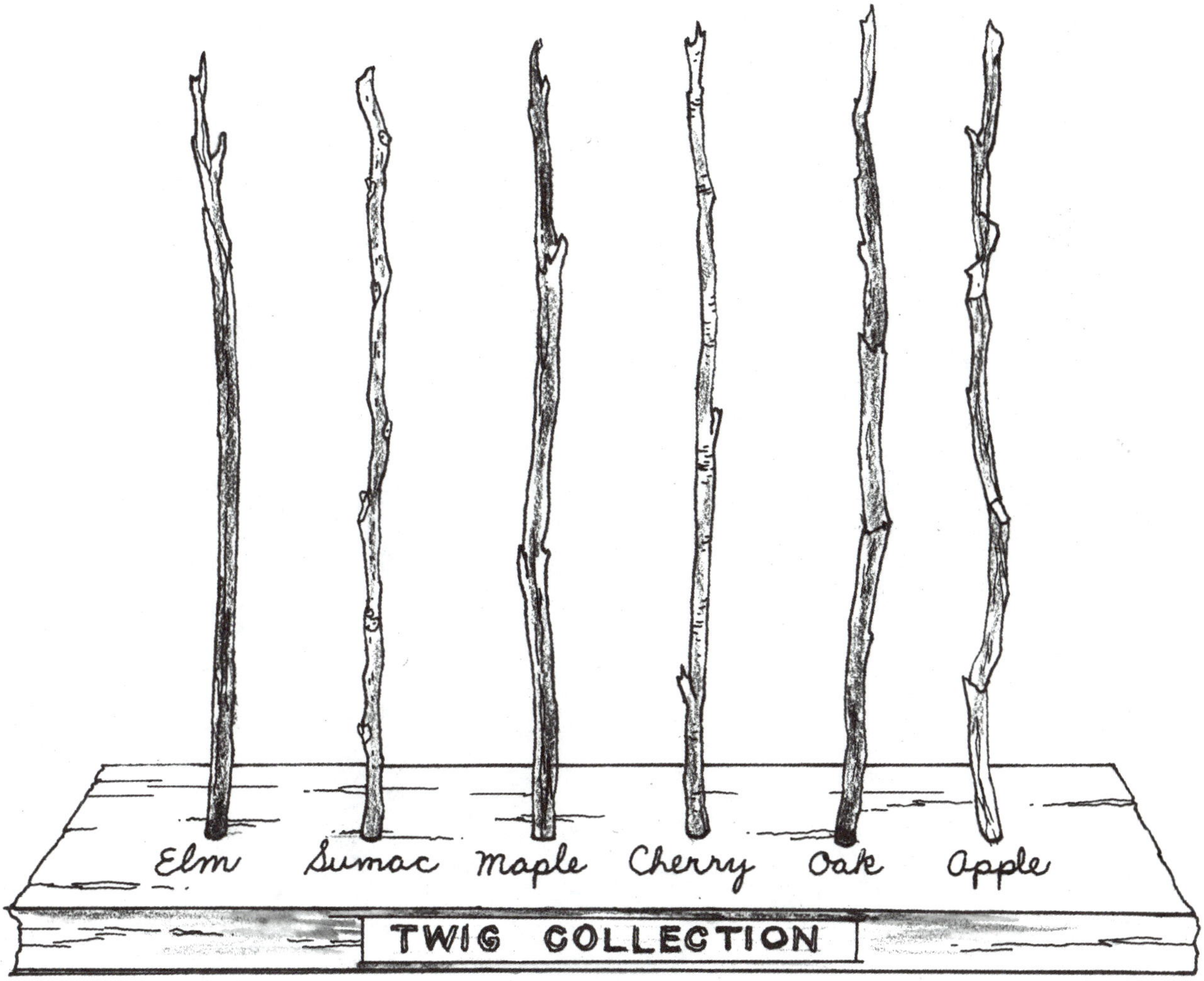

Elm   Sumac   Maple   Cherry   Oak   Apple

TWIG COLLECTION

adult for help. Even without their leaves, trees can be identified by their bark and their shape.

When you cut off a twig, attach a tag to it with a short piece of masking tape. Write on the tape the name and location of the tree.

Before mounting the twigs for display, cut them all the same length, about six inches long. The twigs can be nailed to a block of wood with small brads. Another way to make a twig holder is to drill holes into a piece of wood.

Attach small labels near each twig to show the name and location of the tree from which each came. Keep your twig collection in your room so you can show it to your friends.

MAKING BUDS BLOOM

You can force some kinds of buds to bloom long before spring comes. Cut a few small twigs from different trees. Willow and maple buds are some of the best.

Put the twigs into a glass of water placed in a warm, sunny spot. Each week you should cut off a half-inch piece from the bottom of each twig. The clean cut will make it easier for water to enter the twig.

Remember to look at the buds every few days. Some of the buds may make leaves, while others might turn into little flowers. The large bud on the end of each twig is what grows to make the twig longer in the spring.

COLLECTING PINE CONES

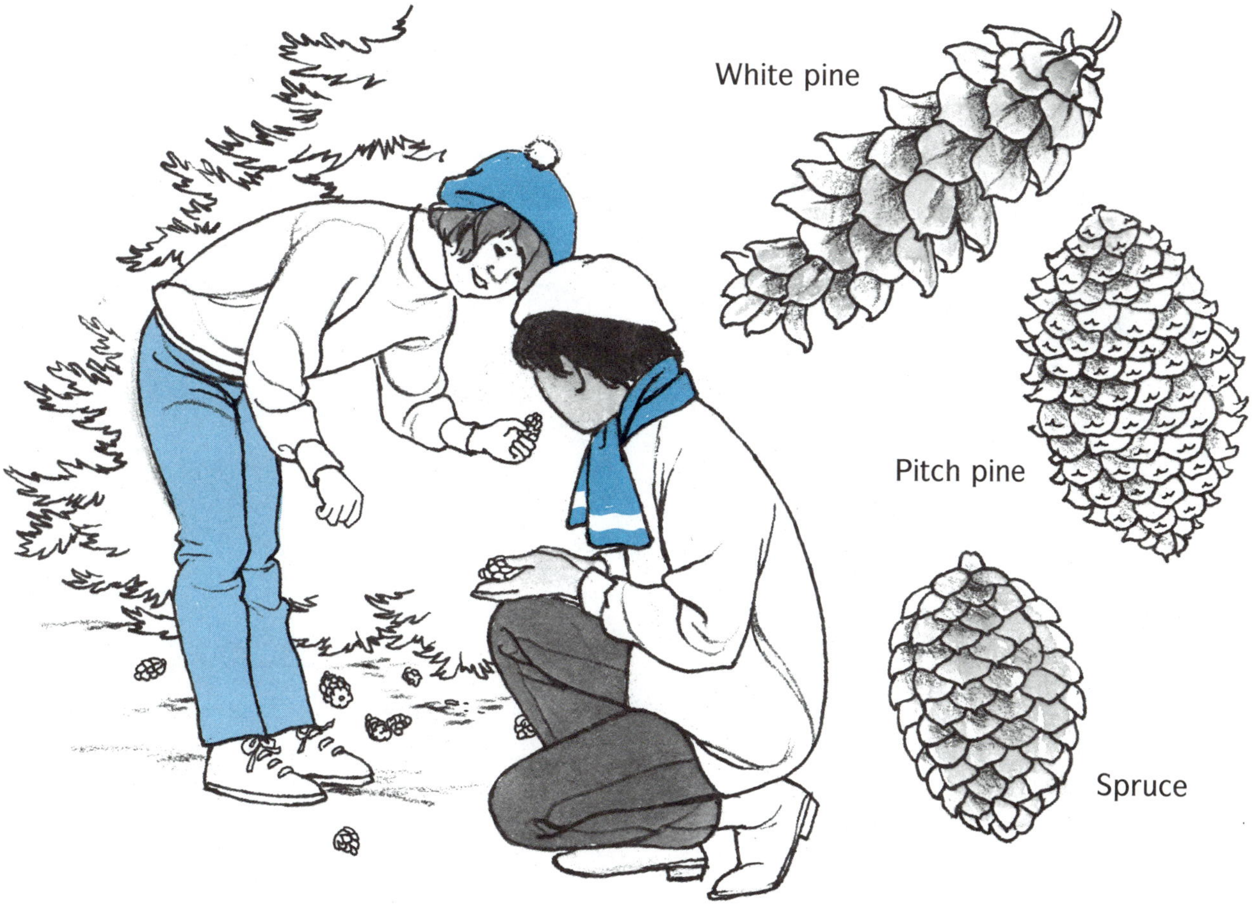

White pine

Pitch pine

Spruce

Evergreen trees in the pine family have needles instead of leaves. And these are the only trees that make their seeds in cones.

How many different kinds of cones can you find? Look in the fallen needles under evergreen trees. In the winter, most cones have dropped from the branches. Try to collect cones from five different evergreen trees.

The cones of white pine are long and narrow, and have thin, rounded scales. Pitch pine cones are quite prickly. Spruce trees have small cones with thin scales. The largest cones come from sugar pines, and can be over twelve inches long.

Ask someone to help you identify the cones you find. A tree guide from the library will help.

GALLS

A gall is a rounded swelling caused by a small fly. The adult fly lays eggs in a plant leaf or stem. As the eggs hatch, the plant swells up around them to form a rounded bump. The larvae feed on plant juices and grow larger inside the gall. Sometimes birds and squirrels tear open galls and eat the larvae.

A good time to look for galls on trees is in the winter when branches are bare. Also look for galls on dead flower stalks in a field. You might find other kinds of galls on fallen aspen or oak leaves.

Look at the outside of a gall. Can you see a hole made when the larvae hatched out? Maybe there are larvae still inside. Have an adult help you cut open the gall with a knife. Larvae look like small, white worms. Can you find any?

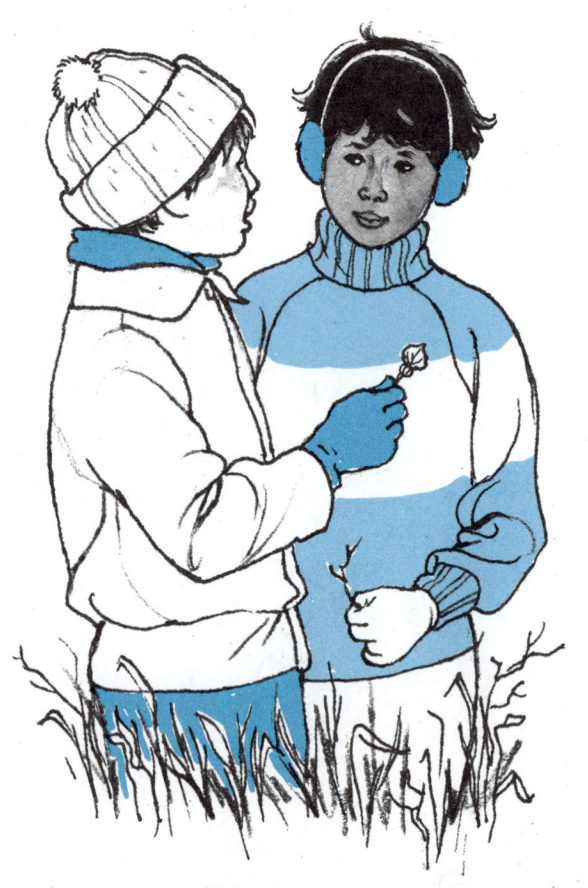

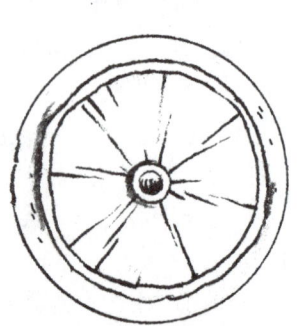

Oak apple gall

Goldenrod gall

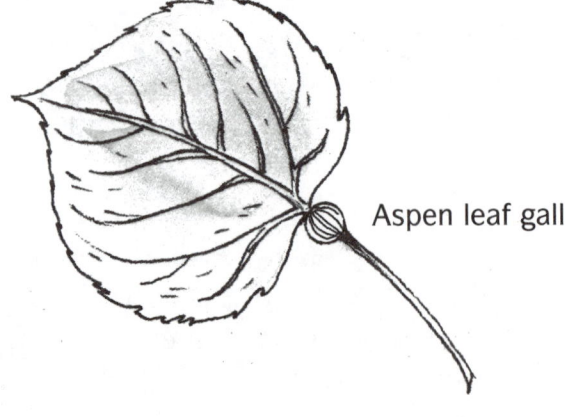

Aspen leaf gall

DEAD LEAVES

You can find leaves even in the winter. Many leaves that dropped from trees in the fall are still on the ground. Slowly, dead leaves rot away and turn into rich soil.

Where would you look for rotting leaves? The wind usually blows leaves into tall grass or underneath bushes. In the woods, dead leaves are left all over the ground.

Use your hands to dig through layers of rotting leaves. Try to find a leaf that is beginning to rot. Maybe you can get a leaf "skeleton" with just the harder veins left.

Dig down and look for leaves on the bottom that have almost turned into soil. If you are lucky, you may find insects hiding from the winter cold in decaying leaves.

Leaf skeleton

A NATURE MUSEUM

Have you ever been to a science museum? You can make a nature museum of your own at home.

You will need a display area, such as a bookshelf or table, on which to arrange things you find and make. You could have your snow goggles, the snow-melting charts, drawings of tracks, feathers, tree buds, galls, and pine cones. Make signs to tell about the nature displays.

Your friends might enjoy seeing your nature museum. Then they will know what you learned outdoors in the winter. Keep your displays and add to them in other seasons of the year.

INDEX

ABOUT THE AUTHOR & ARTIST

David Webster teaches elementary science at the Dexter School in Brookline, Massachusetts. He was a staff member of the elementary science study of the Education Development Center. Mr. Webster has written sixteen science books, including *Frog and Toad Watching* and *How to Do a Science Project*. He lives in Lincoln, Massachusetts, and spends summers on Bailey Island in Maine.

Barbara Steadman studied at the Museum School of Art in Philadelphia and now lives in New York City. She illustrated the *Girl Scout Junior Handbook*.